Marching with Martin

LORENZO PACE

WINDMILL BOOKS

New York

Published in 2015 by The Rosen Publishing Group, Inc.
29 East 21st Street, New York, NY 10010

First Edition

Book Design: Brian Garvey

All artwork by Lorenzo Pace

Library of Congress Cataloging-in-Publication Data

Pace, Lorenzo.
Marching with Martin / by Lorenzo Pace.
p. cm. — (African American quartet)
ISBN 978-1-4777-9285-8 (library binding) — ISBN 978-1-4777-9286-5 (pbk.) — ISBN 978-1-4777-9287-2 (6-pack)
1. King, Martin Luther, Jr., — 1929–1968 — Juvenile literature. 2. African Americans — Civil rights — History — 20th century — Juvenile literature. 3. Civil rights movements — United States — History — 20th century — Juvenile literature. II. Pace, Lorenzo. II. Title.
E185.97.K5 P334 2015
323—d23

Manufactured in the United States of America

Cover and interior pages artwork by Lorenzo Pace, photographed by Cindy Reiman.
Image sources: Cover Julian Wasser/The Life Images Collection/Getty Images; p. 5 Kenneth C. Zirkel/E+/Getty Images; pp. 7, 31 Hulton Archive/Getty Images; p. 9 Robert W. Kelley/The Life Picture Collection/Getty Images; p. 13 Michael Evans/New York Times Co./Archive Photos/Getty Images; p. 15 Underwood Archives/Archive Photos/Getty Images; p. 17 Pictorial Parade/Archive Photos/Getty Images; p. 19 Don Cravens/The Life Image Collection/Getty Images; p. 21 AFP/AFP/Getty Images; p. 23 Robert Abbott Sengstacke/Archive Photos/Getty Images; p. 27 Photo Researchers/Science Source/Getty Images; p. 29 Omikron Omikron/Science Source/Getty Images; p. 33 Morton Broffman/Archive Photos/Getty Images; p. 35 William Lovelace/Express/Hulton Archive/Getty Images; p. 37 Joseph Louw/The Life Images Collection/Getty Images; p. 39 Rolls Press/Popperfoto/Getty Images; p. 43 Timothy A. Clary/AFP/Getty Images; pp. 45, 47 Cindy Reiman

Marching with Martin

Many years ago, in 1949, to be exact, when I was a little boy in Alabama, I saw signs I did not understand.

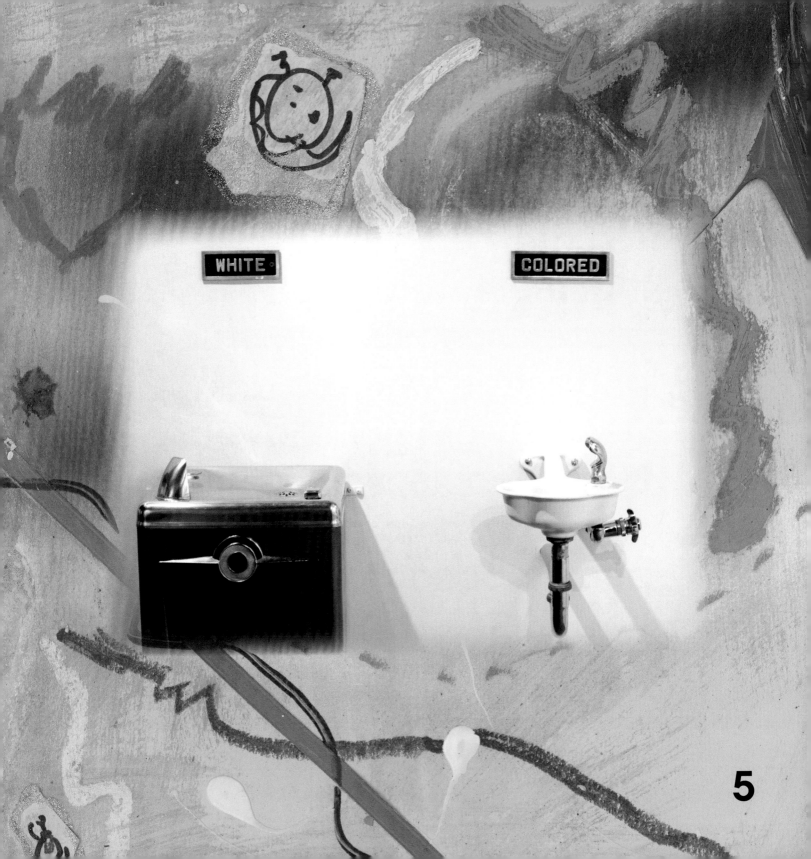

As I grew up, I learned that there were many places, such as restaurants and shops, where black people were not allowed. Black people were kept segregated from white people because of the color of our skin.

7

Many people at that time hated African Americans. They hated us because we wanted our rights as people. We were demanding our civil rights, and some of the people who hated us became violent.

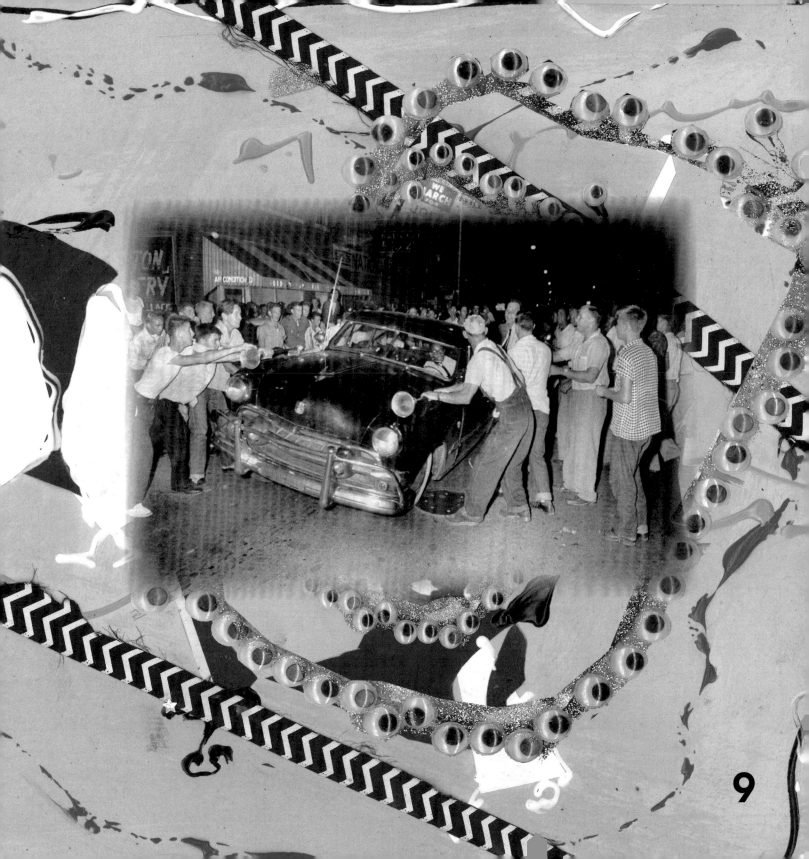

9

My daddy was a preacher. He taught me and my brothers and sisters that the people who hated us were just afraid of change. They were afraid of what they didn't know.

11

There was another preacher in Alabama in the 1950s. He was saying the same things my daddy was saying. His name was Martin Luther King Jr. He was a leader in our protests.

13

On December 2, 1955, a woman named Rosa Parks in Montgomery, Alabama, refused to give up her seat on the bus to a white person. She was arrested. Dr. Martin Luther King Jr. led all the African-American citizens of Montgomery in a nonviolent protest: a boycott. Nobody rode the buses. I felt proud when I heard about it on the news.

When I was 14, my daddy moved our family to Chicago. My mama packed lunch boxes for our journey on the train. We had chicken and ribs and cornbread. All the food of the South we loved. Little did we know that we were leaving the segregated South for the segregated South Side of Chicago. We took the struggle with us.

17

I made a lot of friends in Chicago. All of us admired Dr. King. We admired his courage. Someone tried to kill him, but he survived and would not be silent. An angry mob tried to destroy the church of his friend Reverend Ralph Abernathy but they did not succeed. In Birmingham, Alabama, the police put Dr. King in jail and let dogs attack the protestors. But nothing could stop our demands for justice.

In 1963, I didn't have enough money to go to Washington, D.C., to march with Dr. King. But all of us, my family and friends, watched him on TV. He said,

"I have a dream today. I have a dream that one day, down in Alabama... little black boys and black girls will be able to join hands with little white boys and white girls as sisters and brothers. I have a dream today."

21

He was talking about me, to me, about my childhood, about the future for my children. And then in 1965, Dr. King came to Chicago. I wasn't going to miss that. We were marching for jobs, equal opportunities, human dignity, respect.

23

All my friends came with me: white friends, brown friends, girls, and boys. We were all art students. We were learning to express ourselves with paint and wood and stone. Now with Dr. King we could express ourselves on the street. I was marching with Martin.

KING
MARTIN

Once you feel free to express yourself, you can't stop. You have to say or paint what's on your mind. You can always tell when a person feels that she is free. The great boxer Muhammad Ali was that kind of person. He refused to fight in the American war in Vietnam. His conscience wouldn't let him. I felt that way too. Many young men did.

Dr. King had studied the writings of the Indian leader Mahatma Gandhi. Gandhi wrote, "Only when the chain of hatred is cut can brotherhood begin." In 1967, all my friends and I believed this. We believed in peace and love. We believed in flower power. I wish you could have been there to see how we were changing the world.

No longer did people have to apologize for who they were or how they looked. It was so exciting to understand with all our hearts that BLACK IS BEAUTIFUL. Everyone agreed that Angela Davis had the best 'fro on the planet, and we marched and shouted, "SAY IT LOUD, I'M BLACK AND I'M PROUD!" I made my first sculpture to celebrate us.

Many people joined in marching with Martin: his wife, Coretta Scott King, the Reverends Ralph Abernathy and Fred Shuttlesworth, and many more.

33

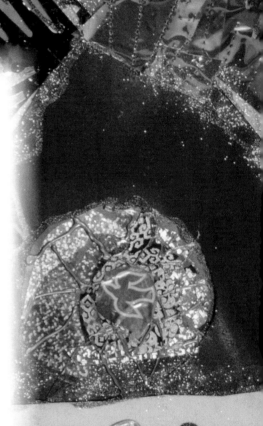

Our marches were changing laws in America: Laws about voting, education, housing, and jobs. In a democracy, the voice of the people will be heard.

And then on April 4, 1968, in Memphis, Tennessee, Dr. King was shot dead by an escaped convict. When I heard the news on the radio, I ran out of my house onto the street. I couldn't breathe. Anger grabbed my throat. And grief squeezed my heart so tight I thought maybe an entire building had fallen on my chest. That feeling lasted a long, long time.

To heal, I had to open my heart to Dr. King's own message of love and unity:

"…All God's children…will be able to join hands and sing… Free at last! Free at last! Thank God almighty, we are free at last!"

And my daddy, Bishop Pace, spoke to me, "Lorenzo, following Dr. King also means being free of hatred, free of suspicion, free of bitterness."

Did we ever arrive at the Promised Land of the fair and just society that we all worked for? No, but we have taken great steps toward this goal. I have lived to see Barack Obama become the first African American president of the United States.

43

I continue to make art in the light of the legacy of Dr. King. Every day, with every step I take, I march with Martin. You can, too. Come on, let's march together.

45

Born in Birmingham, Alabama, Lorenzo Pace spent his adolescence in Chicago, Illinois. He received his BFA and MFA degrees from the School of the Art Institute of Chicago and his doctorate in art education and administration from Illinois State University in Normal, Illinois. Working with a diversity of objects and materials, Lorenzo has exhibited his sculpture and installations and presented his performance art both nationally and internationally.

In 1992, he was presented with the Keys to the City of Birmingham, Alabama, by Mayor Richard Arrington and Birmingham councilmen Leroy "Tuffy" Bandy and Bernard Kincaid. In 2000, Lorenzo's work was included in "Out of Action: Performance Art 1949–1999," an exhibition of the Museum of Contemporary Art, Tokyo. In the 2008 Olympics in Beijing, Lorenzo represented the United States in an exhibition entitled "One World One Dream" at the Sunshine International Museum of Contemporary Art.

In 2011, investigating his family roots in Tuskegee, Alabama, Lorenzo included as part of a permanent historical marker and art installation a bronze replica of the original slave lock that had held his great-grandfather captive. This installation is at the AME Zion Church in Creek Stand, Alabama, one of the oldest existing slave cemeteries in the United States.

In 2013, Lorenzo's work was also part of a site-specific art installation to honor those people who were taken as slaves from Buea, Cameroon. This installation was part of the "Festival of Sounds, Color, and Arts of Africa" in Douala, Cameroon.

In 2014, Lorenzo was invited to participate in "HistoryMakers," a video oral history of contemporary artists, writers, musicians, actors, and dancers that is now part of the permanent collection at the Library of Congress in Washington, D.C.

Lorenzo currently maintains a studio in Brooklyn, New York. He is the sculptor commissioned to create "Triumph of the Human Spirit" for the African Burial Ground Memorial in Foley Square Park in New York City. He is currently a professor of art at the University of Texas–Rio Grande Valley.

Acknowledgments

The last twenty-five years of continuous personal research of my family tree has been a daunting task, but the end result was to find my family's roots. These books are a major part of this ongoing search, and they are dedicated to many family members and friends. Starting with members of the Clark family who are present today: to Uncle Willie Clark Jr. (1909), Aunt Evelyn Clark (1929), and Elnora Clark Peewee (1914) in Birmingham, Alabama. To members who have passed in the Pace family: my resolute uncle Julian Pace (1911–2006), who presented the original slave lock to me, and to my mother Mary A. Pace (1916–1993) and father Bishop Elder Eddie T. Pace (1909–1991).

These books are also dedicated to my children: Shawn, Ezra, Jalani (the namesake for the first book), and Esperanza. Much respect and thanks to my cousin Shari Williams, director of the Ridge Project of Tuskegee, Alabama, for taking on the difficult task of researching my family tree, starting in Creek Stand, Alabama, the original place of the slave lock of Steve Pace. To all my friends and colleagues who encouraged me to keep going and not to give up on my quest to better understand our collective humanity.

To my little brother Ronald Pace, who is an author himself (*Cane Is Able*, 2012), for his invaluable suggestions and support, which enabled these books to come alive. To the great artist, printmaker, and musician Jose William, who gave me my first art exhibition at the South Side Art Center in Chicago and helped me make my first silk-screen quilt print. To my old Chicago friend and entrepreneur Walter Patrick, who in 1989 first suggested that the publishers review the prototype for *Jalani and the Lock*. Without this introduction, the book might not have come to fruition.

To my colleague Professor Leila Hernandez, an excellent graphic designer at the University of Texas–Rio Grande Valley, for her suggestion to use my grandmother's and mother's quilts as part of the visual concept of the Harriet Tubman volume. To Chicago impresario and author Tom Burrell (*Brainwashed*, 2004), who believed in me before I believed in myself, praising my early artwork and collecting it to this day. To Cassandra Griffen, photojournalist, for her gracious contribution in allowing me to use her photograph of Birmingham civil rights icon Fred Shuttlesworth.

To my soul mate, former teacher at the School of the Art Institute of Chicago, and author Ronne Hartfield (*Another Way Home*, 2004), who introduced me to African literature and heritage as a young art student. This self-reflection led me to the African symbol "Sankofa" meaning "in order to understand oneself as a person, you must look back at your past to move forward into the future." Therefore, to start this process, I had to go to the Motherland of all humanity, Africa.

All this could not have happened without the help, support, and understanding of one of my dearest friends, Lamine Gueye, and his very special family in Dakar, Senegal, West Africa. My travels there to one of Africa's largest slave castles in Gorée Island have provided me with invaluable information and research on the early slave trade to the Americas.

To the publisher Roger Rosen, who had the courage and vision to tackle some of America's most sensitive topics. His orchestration and sensitivity to the completion of these books have made me keenly aware of what a privilege it was to collaborate with this forward-thinking human being. To Brian Garvey, a wonderful graphic designer who was completely up to the challenge of creatively manipulating the visual concepts of the books. Finally, to my brothers and sisters in the Pace family: Eddie Jr., Lawrence, Michael, Alfonzo, William, Ronald, Dorothy, Mary, Shirley, and my sweet sister-in-law Yvonne. To all our future children and to the visionaries who believe in the essence of humanity, so that we can all live in peace and love, celebrating our differences on this beautiful planet that we all share.

~ Dr. Lorenzo Pace